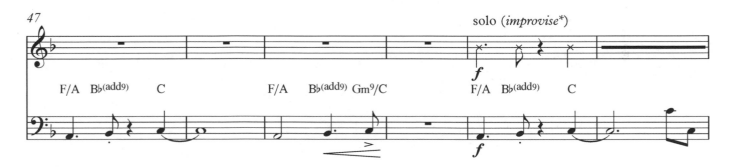

*using chord symbols and initial rhythm as a guide

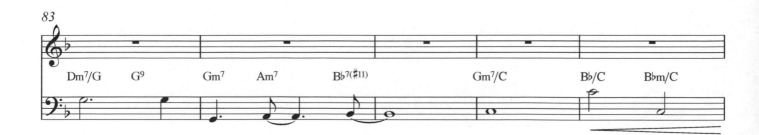

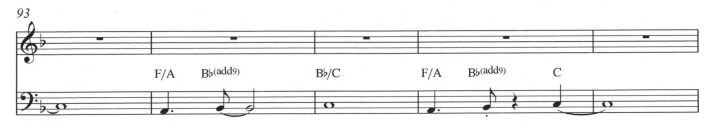

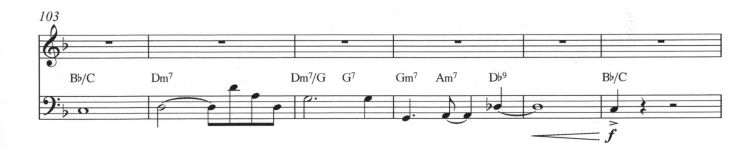

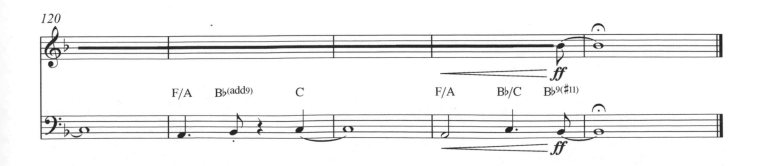

2. Ariel taught me how to play
(Caliban)

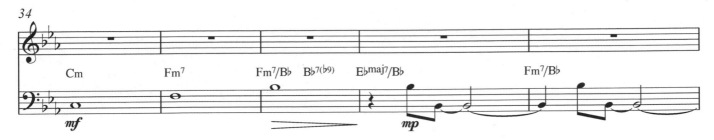

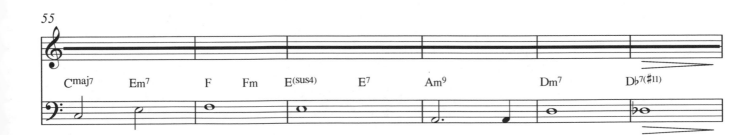

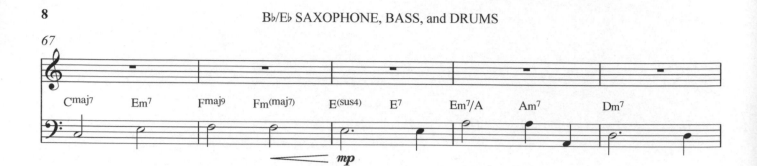

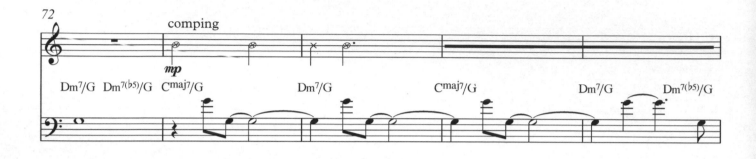

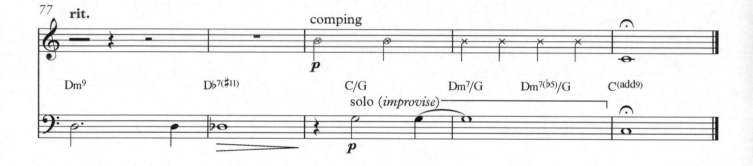

3. *All good things come to an end*
(*Miranda*)

BC190 **Ophelia, Caliban, and Miranda** CHILCOTT

OXFORD

UNIVERSITY PRESS

www.oup.com

ISBN 978-0-19-341272-9

9 780193 412729